The Great Pot of Pressure Cooker Recipes

The most wanted Electric Pressure Cooker Cookbook

Bobby Flatt

Introduction

Taking care of cooking time- this is the first and foremost cooking tip for you, when you are using pressure cooker for cooking a dish. If you increase the cooking time even by one minute then there are chances that your dish will come out over cooked and it is totally true.

To help you out with this critical aspect of cooking, we have a cookbook that will make your cooking journey with pressure cooker easier. Do you want to know how? The answer is that this book contains each and every aspect of pressure cooking in details. There are 25 recipes in this cookbook and each of them contains required cooking time. You will just have to follow the recipe to the toe and work with stopwatch.

You will be overwhelmed with the quality of recipes mentioned in this book. There are flavors from Germany till Jamaica. A chicken dish, a lobster dish, or a pork rib dish, you will find all of them in this cookbook.

We acknowledge the fact that you are living in a social surrounding where you are sometimes required to throw a small get together party for your friends group. This is the reason why we provide you with recipes for course meal, right from starters to desserts and in-between. Also, if you want to add or subtract a few herbs and spices from the original recipe then you can do that, to suit your own taste. You will definitely be impressed by the language and quality of recipes and will want to cook more often with pressure cooker!!

TABLE OF CONTENTS

INTRODUCTION 2

SOUP, STEW & STARTERS 6

CLAM CHOWDER FROM NEW ENGLAND 7

FRENCH SOUPY ONION 9

AWESOME IRISH STEW 12

SUPER DUPER SPAGHETTI SAUCE 15

ITALIAN MYSTERY SOUP 17

VEGETABLES & SIDE DISH 20

BUTTERNUT RISOTTO BEAUTY 21

QUINOA QUEENS PILAF 23

PURE RICE PILAF 25

COCKTAIL CURVY ONIONS 27

MAIN COURSE 29

COOKER MAGIC WITH CHICKEN SAUCE 30

COOKER PERFECT CARNITAS 33

CURRY MAGIC WITH BANGLADESHI BEAUTY 35

BROAD BEANS JAMAICAN FLAVORS 38

BABY RIBS BEAUTY 41

PULLED PORK 43

QUEEN OF CRAB 45

LOBSTER SEA MANIA 47

FROZEN PASTE CHICKEN 49

ASIAN MISTY RICE WITH CHICKEN 51

BEEF STRONG-OFF 53

SHORT SEXY RIBS 55

CANNED FRUITS & DESSERTS 58

CANNED FRUITY PEARS 59

APPLE SLURPY SAUCE 61

CRÈME CRAVALICIOUS BRULEE 63

CRISPY APPLE DESSERT 65

SOUP, STEW & STARTERS

Clam Chowder from New England

Neck clam is the most common ingredient used in preparations in New England. Enjoy this lovely clam chowder on leisurely evening!!

Image Credit: Flickr user Foodistablog,
<https://www.flickr.com/photos/foodista/3632145415/sizes/o/>

Prep Time: 15 min.
Serving Size: 6

INGREDIENTS:

- Little neck - 25 clams
- Butter - 3 tbsp.
- Diced celery - 3 stalk
- Diced bacon – 8 oz.
- Flour - 3 tbsp.
- Onion, peeled -1
- Sprig thyme - 1
- Clam broth - 6 cups
- White diced potatoes - 2
- Heavy cream - 3/4 cups
- Red pepper, diced and seeded - 1/2
- Bay leaves - 2
- Sea salt as required
- Black pepper as required

DIRECTIONS:

1. At first take your electric cooker and place its inner pot. Add in bacon in the given inner pot. Press the rightful function given for making soup or stew. Cook until crisp.
2. Now mix in the butter and then vegetables. Let it cook for about 10-12 minutes. Then after mix in the flour and again cook for the next 2 minutes.
3. Now mix all other ingredients except cream. Stir them well.
4. Now close the lid on top of the Electric cooker, lock it and then close the valve given for pressure release. Press the button given to warm the food. Again press the button given for making soup or stew. Let the timer reach out to zero.
5. Then open the valve to release the entire pressure. After all the steam gets released, take off the lid.
6. At last mix in the cream. Stir it well and serve hot!!

FRENCH SOUPY ONION

French soupy onion is one of the hot favorite one for pressure cooker freaks. It adds healthy value to your dining table with goodness of Swiss cheese, and toasted Italian breads. Sherry is being added to it to bring out more flavors!!

Prep Time: 12 min
Serving Size: 4

INGREDIENTS:

- Diced onions, peeled - 4
- Sprigs thyme - 2
- Beef stock - 32 oz.
- Butter - 3 tbsp.
- Bay leaf - 1
- Black pepper - 1 tsp.
- Sea salt - 1 tsp.
- Swiss cheese - 8 slices
- Toasted Italian bread - 6 slices
- Sherry - 1/2 cup

DIRECTIONS:

1. At first take your electric cooker and place its inner pot. Press the rightful function given for making meat or chicken.
2. Now mix in the onions and butter. Stir in between till all onions cooked nicely and gets caramelized.
3. Then after mix in herbs, sherry and seasoning. Let it cook for 1-2 minute; then after pour in the stock.
4. Press the button given to warm the food. Now close the lid on top of the Electric cooker, lock it and then close the valve given for pressure release.
5. Press the rightful function given for making soup or stew. Now set the timer of the cooker at 12 minutes. Let the timer reach out to zero.
6. Then open the valve to release the entire pressure. After all the steam gets released, take off the lid.
7. On top part mix in the toasted bread, make a layer of cheese over the bread.

8. Put the lid on, close the pressure valve. Press the button given for making fish or vegetable. Let the timer reach out to zero.
9. Then open the valve to release the entire pressure. After all the steam gets released, take off the lid. Serve hot!!

Awesome Irish Stew

Irish stew prepared from lamb leg, is been used since decades in Irish preparations to add rich and aromatic flavors. Prepare this popular stew at home to enjoy all the goodness of beef stock and potatoes!!

Prep Time: 6 1/2 hours
Serving Size: 7-8

INGREDIENTS:

- Flour - 1 cup
- Lamb leg, cubed and boneless - 64 oz.
- Baby potatoes – 16 pieces
- Onions, pearl and peeled – 20 pieces
- Beef stock - 4 cups
- Minced garlic - 8 cloves
- Red wine - 1 cup
- Sprigs rosemary - 2
- Tomato paste - 4 tbsp.
- Carrots, cut to make medium pieces - 6 large
- Bay leaves - 2
- Olive oil - 6 tbsp.
- Black pepper and sea salt as required

DIRECTIONS:

1. At first take the lamb; season it nicely with pepper and salt. Now take medium sized bowl; add in flour (1 cup). Mix seasoned lamb in the bowl and mix it well with flour to coat well.
2. Then after take your electric cooker and place its inner pot. Add in oil in the given inner pot. Press the rightful function given for making chicken or meat.
3. Add the prepared lamb in heating oil; let it cook till gets browned from its sides. Take out the lamb and set aside.
4. In the inner pot; add some vegetables and allow it to cook nicely for the next 5 minutes.
5. Mix in tomato paste and again cook for about 1 minute. Now mix all the entire remaining ingredient and also add the lamb in the pot again.
6. Now close the lid on top of the Electric cooker, lock it and then close the valve for pressure release. Press the button given to

warm the food. Again press the button given for making slow cooker recipes and setout timer to 6 hours. Let the timer reach out to zero.
7. Then open the valve to release the entire pressure. After all the steam gets released, take off the lid and enjoy!!

Super Duper Spaghetti Sauce

This Super Duper Spaghetti Sauce serves flavorful recipe by wrapping garlic, tomatoes, and oregano as key ingredients. The health quotient of the recipe is being added with inclusion of basil in it.

Prep Time: 50 min.
Serving Size: 2-3

INGREDIENTS:

- Tomatoes, crushed - 2 cans
- Garlic, minced - 3 cloves
- Onion, minced - 1/2
- Oregano, chopped - 1/2 tsp.
- Basil, chopped - 1 tbsp.
- Olive oil - 2 tbsp.
- Ground pepper - 1/2 tsp.
- Water - 1/2 cup
- Sea salt - 1 tsp.
- Sugar - 1 tbsp.

DIRECTIONS:

1. At first take your electric cooker and place its inner pot. Press the rightful function given for beef or chicken. Add in garlic and onions in the inner pot and sauté them.
2. Mix all remaining ingredients along with tomatoes and allow it to cook for about 5 min.
3. Carefully fill the jars with prepares sauce, keep 1 inch of space from the top.
4. Use spatula to press sauce in the jar and to release any left-over bubbles. Clean out rims with seal and white vinegar.
5. Now arrange the jars nicely in inner pot. Pour in some water till it covers 1/4 part of the jar.
6. Now close the lid on top of the Electric cooker, lock it and then close the valve for pressure release. Now press the button given for preserving or canning. Adjust time till its 45 min shows. Let the timer reach out to zero.
7. Then open the valve to release the entire pressure. After all the steam gets released, take off the lid. Use canning tongs to take out jars from inner pot.

Italian Mystery Soup

This mystery soup recipe is the gifted recipe to me by my mom, but the current version is bit of tweaked to suit modern taste culture. Prepared in a pressure cooker, it only takes around 20 minutes to get a hearty full meal; you can also freeze it and re-use it later.

Prep Time: 50 min.
Serving Size: 8

INGREDIENTS:

- Olive oil - 2 tbs.
- Garlic, minced - 3 cloves
- Diced Onion - 1 medium
- turkey sausage (Italian) links, with removed casings - 4 pieces
- Green lentils - 1 cup
- Pearl barley - 1/2 cup
- Parsley, chopped - 1/2 cup
- Chicken breast half with removed skin - 1 piece
- Chicken stock - 3 cups
- Spinach leaves - 1 bag of around 16 oz.
- Drained chickpeas - 1 can of 15 oz.
- Mild salsa - 1 cup

DIRECTIONS:

1. At first take your electric cooker and place its inner pot. Add in oil (1 tbs.) in the given inner pot. Press the rightful function given for making soup or stew.
2. Mix sausage meat, and let it cook till becomes brown colored, break them into pieces. Place the sausage in a plate and then drain out all the oil.
3. In the pot, again pour in olive oil (1 tbs.); add in garlic and onion and cook till becomes translucent.
4. Mix barley in it and stir for 1 minute. Pour in the prepared sausage. Mix in chicken, parsley, chicken stock, and lentils in the pot. Add sufficient stock till it covers up all chicken.
5. Now close the lid on top of the Electric cooker, lock it and then close the valve for pressure release. Again press the button given for making soup or stew. Set the cooker's timer to 25 minutes. Let the timer reach out to zero.

6. Then open the valve to release the entire pressure. After all the steam gets released, take off the lid.
7. Take out the chicken; shred out its meat and add them to soup. Mix salsa, spinach, and garbanzo beans; stir the mixture to mix well. Heat again before serving.

VEGETABLES & SIDE DISH

Butternut Risotto Beauty

The popularity of Butternut Risotto is unmatched across highest rated restaurants across USA. It encircles the perfect blend of rise, basil and lots of vegetables.

Prep Time: 10 min.
Serving Size: 7-8

INGREDIENTS:

- White onion, diced and peeled – 1 pieces
- Olive oil - 2 tbsp.
- Chicken broth - 6 cups
- Butternut squash, cubed, seeded & peeled - 2 cups
- Arborio rice - 2 cups
- Butter - 2 tbsp.
- Cheese (Romano), grated - 3 tbsp.
- Chopped Basil - 1 1/2 tbsp.
- Cinnamon- 1 medium stick
- White dry wine - 3/4 cup
- Black pepper and Salt as required

DIRECTIONS:

1. At first take your electric cooker and place its inner pot. Add in butter and oil in the given inner pot. Press the rightful function given for making meat or chicken.
2. After all butter melts completely; mix in the butternut squash and onions. Cook onions for about 4 minutes, stir them in between.
3. Mix wine and rice and wine. Again cook till all wine gets absorbed. Then after, mix in cinnamon stick, chopped basil, salt, and broth.
4. Now close the lid on top of the Electric cooker, lock it and then close the valve for pressure release. Press the button given to warm the food. Now press the button given for rice or risotto. Adjust time till its 10 min shows. Let the timer reach out to zero.
5. Then open the valve to release the entire pressure. After all the steam gets released, take off the lid.
6. Finally add the cheese and then for about 30 seconds stir risotto to melt all the cheese. Serve hot!!

Quinoa Queens Pilaf

Quinoa Queens Pilaf is complete side dish that can be enjoyed with lots of ingredient combination. Feel free to experiment it by adding some of your secret ingredients.

Prep Time: 6 min.
Serving Size: 2

INGREDIENTS:

- Quinoa - 3 cups
- Onion, diced - 1/2
- Bay leaf - 1
- Vegetable or chicken stock - 32 oz.
- Sprig thyme - 1
- Butter - 2 tbsp.

DIRECTIONS:

1. At first take your electric cooker and place its inner pot. Add in butter or oil in the given inner pot. Press the rightful function given for making rice or risotto. Let it cook for the next 2 minutes.
2. In the pot, mix the Quinoa and with butter, coat it nicely. Mix all the leftover ingredients.
3. Now close the lid on top of the Electric cooker, lock it and then close the valve for pressure release. Press the button given to warm the food. Again press the button given for rice or risotto. Let the timer reach out to zero.
4. Then open the valve to release the entire pressure. After all the steam gets released, take off the lid. Enjoy hot!!

Pure Rice Pilaf

Pure Rice Pilaf is among the irresistible mouth-watering side dishes; this side kick creates heavenly fusion of vegetables, and rice. Prepare it in small potion to double its flavors and enjoyment.

Prep Time: 6 min.
Serving Size: 3-4

INGREDIENTS:

- Vegetable or chicken stock - 32 oz.
- Rice - 3 cups
- Butter - 2 tbsp.
- Sprig thyme - 1
- Onion, diced - 1/2
- Bay leaf - 1

DIRECTIONS:

1. At first take your electric cooker and place its inner pot. Add in butter or oil in the given inner pot. Press the rightful function given for making rice or risotto. Let it cook for the next 2 minutes.
2. In the pot, mix in rice and with butter, coat them nicely. Mix in all leftover ingredients.
3. Now close the lid on top of the Electric cooker, lock it and then close the valve for pressure release. Press the button given to warm the food. Again press the button given for making rice or risotto. Let the timer reach out to zero.
4. Then open the valve to release the entire pressure. After all the steam gets released, take off the lid. Serve hot!!

Cocktail Curvy Onions

Cocktail Curvy Onions is a magical side dish to impress guests and friends over thanksgiving. Even if they are tasting it for the first time, they will become fan of it without and doubt.

Prep Time: 20 min.
Serving Size: 6-8

INGREDIENTS:

- Pearl onions - 32 oz.
- Pepper flakes, red - 1 tbsp.
- Sugar - 3/4 cup
- White vinegar - 4 cups
- Pickling spice - 1 tbsp.
- Bay leaves - 2
- Water - 32 oz.
- Mustard seed - 1 tbsp.
- Salt - 1/4 cup

DIRECTIONS:

1. At first take your electric cooker and place its inner pot. Mix in all of the mentioned ingredients (leave out chopped onions) in the given inner pot. Press the rightful function given for making meat or chicken. Let the mixture boil.
2. Now take the jars and fill them with the Pearl Onions. Carefully pour the sauce in the jars, keep 1 inch of space from the top.
3. Use spatula to press sauce in the jar and to release any left-over bubbles. Clean out rims with seal and white vinegar. Now arrange the jars nicely in inner pot. Pour in some water till it covers 1/4 part of the jar.
4. Now close the lid on top of the Electric cooker, lock it and then close the valve for pressure release. Press the button given to preserving or canning the food. Let the timer reach out to zero.
5. Then open the valve to release the entire pressure. After all the steam gets released, take off the lid. Carefully take the jars out with canning tongs.

MAIN COURSE

Cooker Magic with Chicken Sauce

Chicky chicken sauce is an easy to make in pressure cooker. It brings out subtle and tangy taste with goodness of chicken. It suits well with white rice or with stir fried broccoli.

Prep Time: 30 min.
Serving Size: 4

INGREDIENTS:

- Whole chicken, cut to make small pieces - 48 oz.
- Dried marjoram - 1/2 tsp.
- Olive oil - 1 tbs.
- Paprika - 1/2 tsp.
- Chicken broth - 1/4 cup
- White wine - 1/4 cup
- Pepper and salt to taste

Duck sauce:
- White vinegar - 2 tbs.
- Minced ginger root - 1 1/2 tbs.
- Apricot preserves - 1/4 cup
- Honey - 2 tbs.

DIRECTIONS:

1. At first take your electric cooker and place its inner pot. Add in oil in the given inner pot. Press the rightful function given for making chicken recipes.
2. In the pot, add the chicken and cook till turns brown. Take out the chicken and season it with paprika, pepper, salt, and marjoram.
3. Drain the oil; add in chicken broth and wine. Again mix the prepared chicken to the mixture.
4. Now close the lid on top of the Electric cooker, lock it and then close the valve for pressure release. Again press the button given for making chicken recipes. Let the chicken cook for about 8 minutes.

5. Then open the valve to release the entire pressure. After all the steam gets released, take off the lid. Place the chicken in serving plate.
6. In the pot, mix in honey, vinegar, apricot preserves, and ginger. Lock it again and turn on warm button. Let it cook for about 12 minutes. Till sauce becomes thick, add the prepared sauce into chicken plate. Enjoy hot!!

Cooker Perfect Carnitas

Perfect alternative to taco bars! Carnitas easily adapts to a slow cooker technique to bring out rich aromatic flavors of pork. You can also freeze it to be enjoyed again later.

Prep Time: 90 min.
Serving Size: 12

INGREDIENTS:

- Beef broth - 1 1/2 cups
- Canola oil - 3 tbs.
- Onion, chopped – 1 large piece
- Ground cumin - 3 tbs.
- Peppers, chopped - 2 fresh
- Ground coriander - 2 tbs.
- Pork shoulder, boneless and cut to make 1 ½ inch cubes - 3 pounds
- Garlic, chopped - 4 cloves
- Serrano pepper, chopped - 1
- Jalapeno peppers, chopped - 3

DIRECTIONS:

1. At first take your electric cooker and place its inner pot. Add in some oil in the given inner pot. Press the rightful function given for making pork recipes.
2. In the pot, add pork cubes and cook them in the oil till gets brown from its sides. Then after, mix in onion, garlic, coriander, cumin, beef broth, jalapeno, Serrano peppers, and Poblano.
3. Now close the lid on top of the Electric cooker, lock it and then close the valve for pressure release. Press the button given to warm the food. Again press the button given for making pork cuisines. Set its timer to 60-65 minutes. Let the timer reach out to zero.
4. Then open the valve to release the entire pressure. After all the steam gets released, take off the lid. Serve immediately!!

Curry Magic with Bangladeshi Beauty

This spicy & tangy beef curry can be enjoyed best with classic Indian basmati rice; also it goes lovely with pita bread or naan.

Prep Time: 1 hour 15 min.
Serving Size: 6

INGREDIENTS:

- Olive oil - 3 tbs.
- Beef chuck, Boneless, cut to make 1 ½ inch pieces – 32 oz.
- Garlic, minced - 6 cloves
- Cardamom seeds, whole – 3
- Onion, chopped - 1
- Cloves, whole - 2
- Ginger paste - 1 tsp.
- Sliced peppers, Green chile - 5
- Ground cumin - 1 tsp.
- Cinnamon sticks - 1 1/2 of around 2 inch
- Cayenne pepper - 1 tsp.
- Turmeric, Ground - 1 tsp.
- Coriander, Ground - 1 tsp.
- Garlic powder - 1 tsp.
- Water - 1 cup

DIRECTIONS:

1. At first take your electric cooker and place its inner pot. Add in some oil and onions in the given inner pot. Press the rightful function given for making beef recipes. Let the onions cook in oil for about 15 minutes till gets softened.
2. Then after, add in the garlic, cinnamon sticks, ginger paste, green chile, cloves, and cardamom seeds. Cook then till turn brown for about 4-5 minutes.
3. Mix in cumin, turmeric, coriander, cayenne pepper, garlic powder, and water in the pot mixture. Simmer till all water evaporates to make mixture more thick.
4. In the pot mixture, mix in pieces of beef chuck to get evenly coat with spice mixture. Now close the lid on top of the

Electric cooker, lock it and then close the valve for pressure release. Again press the button given for making beef cuisines. Set its timer at 1 hour. Let the timer reach out to zero.

5. Then open the valve to release the entire pressure. After all the steam gets released, take off the lid.

Broad Beans Jamaican Flavors

Broad beans have always been the first choice for healthy protein packed meals. Traditionally made since centuries in Jamaica, the dish is among my grandmother's favorite.

Prep Time: 75 min.
Serving Size: 4

INGREDIENTS:

- Beef oxtail, cut to make small pieces – 16 oz.
- Ginger root, minced - 1 tsp.
- Green onion, thinly and finely sliced - 1
- Onion, chopped - 1
- Freshly chopped thyme - 1
- Minced garlic - 2 cloves
- Soy sauce - 2 tbs.
- Chile pepper, chopped - 1
- Black pepper - 1 tsp.
- Salt - 1/2 tsp.
- Water - 1 ½ cups
- Vegetable oil - 2 tbs.
- Allspice berries, whole - 1 tsp.
- Fava beans, canned & drained - 1 cup
- Cornstarch - 1 tbs.

DIRECTIONS:

1. Take large mixing bowl; mix in oxtail with the onion, pepper, salt, ginger, green onion, chile pepper, garlic, thyme, and soy sauce.
2. Now take your electric cooker and place its inner pot. Add in prepared oxtail mixture and water (1 ½ cup) in the given inner pot. Press the rightful function given for making main course recipes. Cook for the next 10 minutes.
3. Now close the lid on top of the Electric cooker, lock it and then close the valve for pressure release. Again press the button given for making main course meals. Set cooker's timer at 25 minutes. Let the timer reach out to zero.
4. Then open the valve to release the entire pressure. After all the steam gets released, take off the lid.

5. Then after, mix in the allspice berries and fava beans. Take water (2 tbs.) in separate container, add cornstarch in it; dissolve well and add it to oxtail mixture. Press the button given to warm the food. Cook for another 4-5 minutes or till the sauce thickens up nicely and beans becomes nicely tender.

Baby Ribs Beauty

Baby rib is the basic ingredient of this main course and when it is mixed with barbeque sauce it creates heaven for pressure cooker lover. When you will cook this one in pressure cooker, then you will get to know the real difference between this lovely one and other ribs preparations.

Prep Time: 40 min.
Serving Size: 4-5

INGREDIENTS:

- Back ribs, small - 3 racks
- Cumin - 1 tbsp.
- Coriander - 1 tbsp.
- Onion powder - 2 tbsp.
- Fine garlic powder - 4 tbsp.
- Onion, diced and peeled - 1
- Barbecue sauce - 2 cups
- Water - 1 cup

DIRECTIONS:

1. At first take mixing bowl, mix in onion powder, garlic powder, coriander, and cumin to season them well. Now take racks and make half pieces of it. Season them well with blend we prepared.
2. Now take your electric cooker and place its inner pot. Add in ribs in the given inner pot. Mix chopped onion and BBQ sauce in the pot to mix well with ribs.
3. Now close the lid on top of the Electric cooker, lock it and then close the valve for pressure release. Press the button given to make soup or stew. Set the cooker's timer till 30-35 min. Let the timer reach out to zero.
4. Then open the valve to release the entire pressure. After all the steam gets released, take off the lid.
5. With BBQ sauce left in pot, nicely brush all the ribs. Serve hot!!

Pulled Pork

Pulled pork has a balanced nutritional values as well as the taste. The BBQ sauce used in this dish gives out of the world delight to taste buds. Get ready to enjoy one of the finest pork delicacies!!

Prep Time: 10 hours.
Serving Size: 10-12

INGREDIENTS:

- Pork shoulder, boneless – 64 oz.
- BBQ sauce, smoky one - 12 oz.
- Cumin - 1 tsp.
- Water - 3 cups
- Cayenne pepper - 1/2 tsp.
- Coriander - 1 tsp.
- Chopped medium onion - 1
- Hamburger rolls
- Salt

DIRECTIONS:

1. At first take your electric cooker and place its inner pot. Add in all the given ingredients (Leave out hamburger rolls and BBQ sauce) in the given inner pot. Press the rightful function given for slow cooking to set the timer at 10 hours.
2. Now close the lid on top of the Electric cooker, lock it and then close the valve for pressure release. Let the timer reach out to zero.
3. Then open the valve to release the entire pressure. After all the steam gets released, take off the lid.
4. Take out the pork; use fork to shred meat, and pour BBQ sauce over it.
5. Enjoy with hamburger rolls.

Queen of Crab

This winner recipe is queen for crab foodie. The delicious crab on melted butter makes it one of the favorite to have on special day. Any quantity of it will not be sufficient enough!!

Prep Time: 3 min.
Serving Size: 12

INGREDIENTS:

- Crab Legs, King size – 64 oz.
- Melted butter - 1/4 cup
- Water - 1 cup
- Lemon wedges - 3

DIRECTIONS:

1. At first take the crab legs; make half pieces of them.
2. Then take your electric cooker and place its inner pot. Add in crab legs and water in the given inner pot.
3. Now close the lid on top of the Electric cooker, lock it and then close the valve for pressure release. Press the button given for making vegetable or fish food. Then set out cooker timer at 4 min. Let the timer reach out to zero.
4. Then open the valve to release the entire pressure. After all the steam gets released, take off the lid. Enjoy with lemon wedges and melted butter.

Lobster Sea Mania

Another sea food preparation but it includes lobster, which is quick to prepare and more importantly gives hassle free cooking experience. Great one for sea food beginners!!

Prep Time: 5 min.
Serving Size: 12

INGREDIENTS:

- Lobsters - 5 pieces of 16 oz. Each
- Melted butter for dipping - 1/4 cup
- White wine - 1/2 cup
- Water - 1 cup

DIRECTIONS:

1. At first take your electric cooker and place its inner pot. Add in wine, lobster and wine in the given inner pot.
2. Now close the lid on top of the Electric cooker, lock it and then close the valve for pressure release. Press the button given to make vegetable or fish recipes. Then set the time of the cooker at 5 min. Let the timer reach out to zero.
3. Then open the valve to release the entire pressure. After all the steam gets released, take off the lid. Enjoy it with dipping of melted butter.

Frozen Paste Chicken

Chicken & pasta dishes are easy one but has the potential to compete with finest of pasta cuisines. This chicken recipe is somewhat different from other chicken dishes and surely deserves to be try-out at least once.

Prep Time: 20 min.
Serving Size: 4

INGREDIENTS:

- Tomato sauce - 24 oz.
- Your choice of favorite pasta - 8 oz.
- Pepper and sea salt as required
- Chicken breasts, frozen – 4 breasts
- Bay leaf - 1
- Chopped basil (optional)

DIRECTIONS:

1. At first take your electric cooker and place its inner pot. Add in all of the mentioned ingredients in the given inner pot.
2. Now close the lid on top of the Electric cooker, lock it and then close the valve for pressure release. Press the button given to make soup or stew. Now set out the cooker's timer at 20 min. Let the timer reach out to zero.
3. Then open the valve to release the entire pressure. After all the steam gets released, take off the lid. Garnish the dish with cheese and basil. Enjoy!!

Asian Misty Rice with Chicken

This is a classic Asian fusion of rice and chicken; something that typically Asian food lovers won't miss out. This one has been twisted a little to suit western flavor.

Prep Time: 7 min.
Serving Size: 4

INGREDIENTS:

- Chicken breasts, skinless, cubed and boneless - 2
- White rice - 1 cup
- Minced ginger - 1 tsp.
- Green pepper, diced and seeded - 1
- Garlic, minced and peeled - 1 clove
- Chicken stock - 1 3/4 cup
- Oil of grape seed - 2 tbsp.
- Chopped scallions - 3
- Broccoli florets - 1 cup
- Onion, diced – 1 medium piece
- Pepper and sea salt as required
- Mixed vegetables - 1 bag

DIRECTIONS:

1. At first take the chicken and season it nicely with black pepper and salt.
2. Then after take your electric cooker and place its inner pot. Add in some oil, vegetables, and chicken in the given inner pot. Press the rightful function given for making meat or chicken. Cook the chicken for about 2 minutes to make it soft.
3. Now mix rice and all other ingredients in the pot.
4. Now close the lid on top of the Electric cooker, lock it and then close the valve for pressure release. Press the button given to warm the food. This time press the button given for making rice or risotto. Let the timer reach out to zero.
5. Then open the valve to release the entire pressure. After all the steam gets released, take off the lid.

Beef Strong-off

Until there is at least one inclusion of beef cuisine that anyone can make in typical fashion, any cook book is incomplete. The beef cuisine is tasty and healthy one to have anytime of the day!!

Prep Time: 10 min.
Serving Size: 4-6

INGREDIENTS:

- Sliced beef, filet or sirloin - 32 oz.
- Beef stock - 2 cups
- Sliced clean mushrooms – 16 oz.
- Bay leaf - 1
- Sour cream - 1/4 cup
- Minced shallot – 1 piece
- Sprig thyme - 1
- Butter - 3 tbsp.

DIRECTIONS:

1. At first take your electric cooker and place its inner pot. Add in butter and beef in the given inner pot. Press the rightful function given for making meat or chicken. Cook till beef turns completely brown from all sides.
2. Now mix in other remaining ingredients (left out sour cream).
3. Now close the lid on top of the Electric cooker, lock it and then close the valve for pressure release. Press the button given to warm the food. Again press the button given for making soup or stew. Let the timer reach out to zero.
4. Then open the valve to release the entire pressure. After all the steam gets released, take off the lid. Pout sour cream over prepared dish and serve hot!!

Short Sexy Ribs

If you are planning to make this sexy rib cuisine then it is advisable to take a leave on your next day as it is going to fill your stomach like nothing. It creates good combination of beef stock with trimmed ribs!!

Prep Time: 45 min.
Serving Size: 6

INGREDIENTS:

- Beef stock - 2 cups
- Short trimmed ribs - 8 pieces
- Tomato paste - 2 tbsp.
- Diced celery - 2 stalks
- Onion, diced - 1 medium
- Garlic, minced - 3 cloves
- Olive oil - 2 tbsp.
- Diced carrots – 2 pieces
- Potatoes, small and red - 8
- Sprig rosemary - 1
- Black pepper - 1 tbsp.
- Bay leaf - 1
- Sprig thyme - 1
- Sea salt - 1 tbsp.

DIRECTIONS:

1. At first take short Ribs and season them nicely with pepper and salt.
2. Then take your electric cooker and place its inner pot. Add in olive oil and ribs in the given inner pot. Press the rightful function given for making meat or chicken. Cook till ribs become brown from its sides.
3. Now take out the prepared ribs and keep aside. Mix in garlic and vegetables. Let them sauté for the next 5 minutes and then mix the paste in it. Again add the ribs and other ingredients in the inner pot.
4. Now close the lid on top of the Electric cooker, lock it and then close the valve for pressure release. Press the button given to warm the food. Again press the button given for making soup

or stew. Set the timer at 40 min. Let the timer reach out to zero.
5. Then open the valve to release the entire pressure. After all the steam gets released, take off the lid. Take out ribs in the serving plate and enjoy!!

CANNED FRUITS & DESSERTS

Canned Fruity Pears

Surprise your guests with fruity pears made in pressure cooker. This colorful lovely dessert will fill up your tummy with rich flavors of pears all over!!

Prep Time: 25 min.
Serving Size: 2

INGREDIENTS:

- Pears, cored & peeled - 6
- Water - 2 cups
- Sugar - 3/4 cup

DIRECTIONS:

1. At first take your electric cooker and place its inner pot. Add in water and sugar in the given inner pot. Press the rightful function given for making meat or chicken. Start boiling the water for 2-3 minutes.
2. Take the pears and make quart pieces from it. Arrange them in the jars.
3. Carefully fill the jars with pears syrup, keep 1 inch of space from the top.
4. Use spatula to press sauce in the jar and to release any left-over bubbles. Clean out rims with seal and white vinegar.
5. Now arrange the jars nicely in inner pot. Pour in some water till it covers 1/4 part of the jar.
6. Now close the lid on top of the Electric cooker, lock it and then close the valve for pressure release. Press the button given to preserving or canning the food. Set cooker's timer to 20 minutes. Let the timer reach out to zero.
7. Then open the valve to release the entire pressure. After all the steam gets released, take off the lid. Use the canning tongs to take out jars from the pot.

Apple Slurpy Sauce

Slurpy apple sauce is the modern dessert incarnation made in pressure cooker. Enjoy this classic saucy dessert anytime and surprise yourself!!

Prep Time: 25 min.
Serving Size: 4-5

INGREDIENTS:

- Apples, halved and cored - 8
- Water - 1/2 cup
- Lemon juice - 1/2
- Sugar - 1/2 cup
- Cinnamon stick - 1

DIRECTIONS:

1. At first take your electric cooker and place its inner pot. Add in all the ingredients of the recipe in the given inner pot. Press the rightful function given for making vegetable or fish. Start cooking them for the next 5 minutes.
2. After all pressure gets released, open the lid and then mash all the applesauce.
3. Carefully fill the jars with applesauce, keep 1 inch of space from the top.
4. Use spatula to press sauce in the jar and to release any left-over bubbles. Clean out rims with seal and white vinegar.
5. Now arrange the jars nicely in inner pot. Pour in some water till it covers 1/4 part of the jar.
6. Now close the lid on top of the Electric cooker, lock it and then close the valve for pressure release. Press the button given to preserving or canning the food. Set cooker's timer to 20 minutes. Let the timer reach out to zero.
7. Then open the valve to release the entire pressure. After all the steam gets released, take off the lid. Use the canning tongs to take out jars from the pot.

Crème Cravalicious Brulee

Crème brulee is the perfect dessert deal for any kind of full course meal. The goodness of egg and crème along with vanilla will leave you and your guests mesmerized!!

Prep Time: 3 1/2 hour.
Serving Size: 4

INGREDIENTS:

- Heavy cream, warm - 2 cups
- Egg yolks - 4
- Vanilla extract - 1 tsp.
- Sugar - 3/4 cup
- Warm water - 1 cup
- Sugar - 3 tsp.

DIRECTIONS:

1. At first take 4 baking dish of 4 oz. capacity; mix in all of the mentioned ingredients (leave out sugar (3 tbs.) and warm water) equally in those baking dishes. Then wrap it nicely by aluminum foil.
2. Now take your electric cooker and place its inner pot. Add in warm water of around 1 cup the given inner pot. Then arrange baking dishes in it.
3. Now close the lid on top of the Electric cooker, lock it and then close the valve for pressure release.
4. Press the button given to make vegetable or fish food. Set cooker's timer to 4-5 minutes. Let the timer reach out to zero.
5. Then open the valve to release the entire pressure. After all the steam gets released, take off the lid.
6. Carefully take out baking dishes and then put it for refrigeration for the next 3 hours.
7. Take out chilled dishes, top them with sugar and then put it under the broiler for sugar caramelization.
8. Enjoy it with fresh berries!!

CRISPY APPLE DESSERT

This yummy crispy dessert fits just perfectly to maintain your total diet intake by being low fat one. Yummy apple takes its divine beauty to another level.

Prep Time: 20s min.
Serving Size: 2

INGREDIENTS:

- Apples, sliced and cored - 4
- Flour - 1/4 cup
- Sea salt - 2/3 tsp.
- Brown sugar - 1/4 cup
- Oats, old-fashioned - 1/2 cups
- Butter - 4 tbsp.
- Ground cinnamon - 2 tsp.
- Lemon juice - 1 1/3 tbsp.
- Warm water - 1 cup
- Ice cream (Optional)

DIRECTIONS:

1. At first take medium bowl, add in lemon juice and apples. Now take another bowl, mix in oats, cinnamon, flour, salt, butter, and brown sugar.
2. Take baking dish; start arranging it. Make first layer of apples and then second with oat crisp mixture. Cover it with foil.
3. At first take your electric cooker and place its inner pot. Add in warm water (1 cup) in the given inner pot. Then arrange prepared baking dishes in it.
4. Now close the lid on top of the Electric cooker, lock it and then close the valve for pressure release. Press the button given to make beans or lentils cuisines. Set the timer of the cooker to 15 minutes. Let the timer reach out to zero.
5. Then open the valve to release the entire pressure. After all the steam gets released, take off the lid. Take out the Apple Crisp and remove foil from it. Let them stand and serve hot!!

Printed in Great Britain
by Amazon